MEDIA LITERACY™

ETHICS
AND DIGITAL
CITIZENSHIP

MEGAN FROMM, Ph.D.

rosen publishing's
rosen
central®

NEW YORK

Published in 2015 by The Rosen Publishing Group, Inc.
29 East 21st Street, New York, NY 10010

First Edition

Library of Congress Cataloging-in-Publication Data

Fromm, Megan.
Ethics and digital citizenship/Megan Fromm.—First edition.
    pages cm.—(Media literacy)
Includes bibliographical references and index.
ISBN 978-1-4777-8066-4 (library bound)
1. Media literacy—Juvenile literature. I. Title.
P96.M4F76 2015
302.23—dc23

2014009712

Manufactured in Malaysia

CONTENTS

INTRODUCTION

A rogue National Security Agency employee living somewhere in Russia. Crowdsourced images of protest in the Middle East. A website publishing state secrets and illegally obtained classified documents. A Twitter revolution. Government-run programs to access phone records and network data. These are the fearful realities and hopeful benefits of a digital world. They demonstrate a new level of civic engagement for the average citizen, and they demand an even greater role for today's journalists. Simply put, they are the reason news still matters.

As the lines between information, advocacy, and rumor blur, the need for news that is accurate, contextual and meaningful has never been greater. We may not yet agree on who is a journalist, but we know that without truthful information, the very function of our democratic society is compromised.

Civic participation requires more than a Facebook "share" or a "like." Instead, these mediums are ideal for organizing and disseminating information about further civic or social action.

In a 1962 speech to employees of federal broadcasting arm Voice of America, President John F. Kennedy remarked on the changing nature of media and storytelling. His remarks, though spoken more than fifty years ago, remain applicable even today:

"For in the next 20 years your problem and ours as a country, in telling our story, will grow more complex. The choices we present to the world will be more difficult, and for some the future will seem even more empty of hope and progress. The barrage upon truth will grow more constant, and some people cannot bear the responsibility of a free choice which goes with self-government. And finally, shrinking from choice, they turn to those who prevent them from choosing, and thus find in a kind of prison, a kind of security."[1]

In advocating for Voice of America's journalistic role, Kennedy described to his audience a press that, if practiced today, would represent a robust exchange of ideas: "We seek a free flow of information across national boundaries and oceans, across iron curtains and stone walls. We are not afraid to entrust the American people with unpleasant facts, foreign ideas, alien philosophies, and competitive values. For a nation that is afraid to let its people judge the truth and falsehood in an open market is a nation that is afraid of its people."

While the iron curtains and stone walls of Kennedy's era have been replaced by fiber optic and broadband cables of a digital age, the necessity of truth and an open market remain the same. Educators, policymakers, and even parents are struggling today with how best to teach students about this "new" media that is, strangely enough, no longer all that new. This requires new approaches for responsible use of digital technology, an emphasis on the difference between fact and fiction, and an ongoing exploration of the role of bias and credibility. And while there is no easy answer, scholastic journalism provides a natural starting point for understanding a revolutionary media world.

Journalism has faced its share of change in recent history, and there is likely more on the horizon. But just as the digital camera has improved both amateur and professional photography, the digital revolution has challenged both journalists and average citizens. What we consider news is shifting dramatically, and the ways in which we receive, digest, and disseminate information must adapt to changing technology.

However, the basic premise of journalism—bringing information of high public value to the masses—is a stable and necessary practice. Where that information comes from, how citizens process it, and what we ultimately choose to do with it in our lives is now determined largely by technology. For young media users, especially, news production and consumption is taking on a whole new meaning and purpose.

CHAPTER ONE

THE IMPORTANCE OF THE NEWS

People born in the age of digital media access are often called digital natives because they have never known life without this technology. Adults, on the other hand, are referred to as digital converts or digital immigrants because they transitioned to digital technology over the course of their lifetime.

Researchers have spent significant time and resources analyzing differences in knowledge, engagement, and disposition between digital natives and digital converts. They are specifically concerned with how much time digital natives spend using media and for what purposes. Of course, this research has shifted focus as new technologies emerge.

However, one phenomenon has remained consistent: Students and young adults spend countless hours with technology, digesting media in digital bites with an appetite greater than ever. According to the Pew Research Center, 95 percent of teenagers were online by 2012.[2] What's more, a Kaiser Family Foundation study found that students age eight to eighteen spend almost eight hours a day tethered to the Internet via smartphones, laptops, or

Digital natives are those who have grown up experiencing digital technology in a variety of mediums. Digital converts, like most adults, must learn to master emerging technology over time.

televisions.[3] Simply put, we're more connected than we've ever been. But what, exactly, are we *doing* online?

Games, entertainment media, and connecting with friends are among the top reasons students use the Internet. Still others refuse to log off for fear of being bored or missing out on something. A recent study found that when 800 students from across the world were asked to disconnect from their mobile phones for 24 hours, many of them reported major symptoms of anxiety.[4]

Consider this response from one of the students in the study: "The mobile phone has become a part of us: our best friend who will save all our secrets, pleasures and sorrows." Another student in the same study reflected on how a virtual connection builds upon real-time connections: "When I am texting or on Facebook, or reading the news, I feel connected to the world rather than just what I am surrounded by at that moment."

FROM "CITIZEN" TO "NETIZEN"

"Netizens," or "cybercitizens," are those people who use the Internet as a primary means of becoming active citizens in their city, state, or nation, or even across the world. They are children, teenagers, and adults who use the Internet to become more responsible, engaged people. This might mean using social media to encourage others to vote, organizing a clothing or food drive online, or even reading different news websites to stay abreast of what's happening in the world.

Teenagers and university students in Chile, for instance, have been using Twitter since 2011 to stage massive protests demanding access to more affordable education. These protests, some attracting more than 100,000 participants, were often organized in 140 characters or less via the Twitter accounts of protest leaders. In 2013, one of those protest leaders, a young college student, was elected to Chilean government.

Social media tools such as Facebook and Twitter have been helpful in mobilizing citizens from around the world to specific social or political concerns.

Of course, one of the most prominent examples of how young adults have used new media to fuel social change is the Arab Spring, the revolutionary demonstrations for democracy across the Arabian Peninsula and North Africa in 2010.

In the United States, immigrant students used Facebook to help highlight the proposed DREAM (Development, Relief, and Education for Alien Minors) Act, a bill that would allow young children brought illegally to the United States to defer deportation so they can finish their education.

Traditionally, these kinds of topics were most often discussed in newspapers and on cable television. Now, anyone can participate in the most important debates of our time with the click of a button. Still, professional journalism plays a vital role in our democracy.

DIGITAL CONNECTIVITY

For many people, digital connectivity is a lifeline, sometimes replacing traditional face-to-face interaction while other times allowing those interactions to flourish and be maintained over time and distance. This is the catch-22, or dilemma with no escape, of digital media—it enables us to disconnect as quickly as it enables us to reconnect. Sometimes, a virtual connection is not as strong as one made in the flesh.

Though many adults are concerned by the amount of time teenagers spend online, recent political events have demonstrated how young adults are using the Internet to become more civically aware and to engage in social, political, and humanitarian issues.

CHAPTER TWO

A WATCHDOG ON A DIGITAL LEASH

For decades, journalists have described themselves as the "watchdog" of politics and the media itself. This metaphor highlights a specific role of news media: to inform citizens of what is happening in government so that we can make the best decisions for our own lives. In *The Press*, scholars W. Lance Bennett and William Serrin note just how significant this role is among journalists' many tasks:

> Watchdog, record keeper, coauthor of history, citizen's guide to action, purveyor of daily social sensation: all of the above are part of the job description of the American Press, and have been for some time. But what is the proper role of the press in a democracy? Of all the established functions of the press in American public life, the watchdog role is among the most hallowed.

James Madison, an architect of the Bill of Rights and later president of the United States, believed that an emerging nation needed a robust and independent press.

The "watchdog" role often means that journalists should scrutinize what is happening in government by keeping close tabs on our public officials and the business they conduct on our behalf. After all, we elected these officials, and journalists can help hold them accountable by telling us what they are doing. Then, we can make up our own minds about whether their actions are right or wrong or whether they are doing the best job in their elected positions.

Founding Father James Madison, in trying to convince Virginia delegates of the need for a Bill of Rights, once said the great danger of a republic is that "the majority may not sufficiently respect the rights of the minority." In this way, the press could help protect minority ideas and rights by keeping an eye on how the government—elected by the majority—is conducting business. Were something to go awry, he expected the press to sound the alarm so that citizens could demand action.

THE PRESS AS THE WATCHDOG

Over time, the press has fulfilled its watchdog role in many ways. In *The Race Beat*, authors Gene Roberts and Hank Kilbanoff discuss just how instrumental news media were in the civil rights movement. The authors quote civil rights leader John Lewis's description of how the press created momentum and paved the way for a more equal nation: "If it hadn't been for the media—the print media and television—the Civil Rights movement would have been like a bird without wings, a choir without a song."

When the press fails to properly execute its role as watchdog, when facts, context, and a thorough evaluation of circumstances slip through the cracks, the results can be devastating. In the lead-up to the Iraq War in 2003, mainstream media failed to investigate claims that the country held weapons of mass destruction, and sweeping administrative statements about connections to al Qaeda went unquestioned.[5]

Today, the "modern notion of a political journalism which is adversarial, critical and independent of the state," as described by media scholar Brian McNair in *The Handbook of Journalism Studies*, is increasingly more difficult in a digital age but still essential for democracy.

While the Internet has created an infinite platform for media coverage, the digital leash of today's watchdog journalist is increasingly short. Why? Because watchdog journalism, which is inherently political, is often enjoyed and sought out by only a select audience.

The kind of watchdog news that was once displayed in front-page glory on street corners is now often buried within a web page. More often than not, you must seek out this kind of news; it doesn't just land in your lap (or on your doorstep) anymore.

the
lion's tale

charles e. smith jewish day school • 11710 hunters lane, rockville, maryland
thursday, may 2, 2013 • vol. 30 issue 7

There are 8 hours until morning.

NETFLIX

hulu

How will you spend them?

Procrastination: Page 12

Information overload can be both caused by and managed through the many technological platforms available today. Knowing which to use, when, and for what purpose is a new requirement of digital citizenship.

This information overload is a common challenge in the digital age. We used to imagine news media, especially newspapers, as being gatekeepers of information. Journalists and editors sifted through all the day's events and decided which were most relevant and important for us based on a number of factors. Now, with hundreds of thousands of information sources publishing on a never-ending cycle, the gatekeeping role has almost disappeared. In its wake, citizens are left to decide what to do with the vast amounts of information streaming at them twenty-four hours a day.

INFORMATION ISN'T ALWAYS NEWS

Watchdog journalism is more important than ever: In a digital world, with news fragmented across multiple media websites, it's easy for important information to slip under the radar. The local city hall that posts minutes of its official business online is doing citizens and journalists a favor with this easy access, but the burdensome amount of information someone has to sift through to find out what's actually happening often turns people away.

Watchdog journalism assumes that some information, or news content, is more important than others. It assumes that reporting on a government shutdown, for example, is more important than a celebrity breakup, a major act of violence trumps the winners of the *American Idol* reality-TV show, and topics such as education, health care, security, poverty, and injustice are worth investigating every day, not just when a journalist gets around to it.

Digital media—and the endless number of media sources online—has challenged this assumption and forced journalists and publishers to work harder to tell these stories. Whether and how these stories are told matters greatly because they are the stories that shape public opinion on how our city, country, and world operates. Journalists seek out facts, construct stories, and in turn become "sensemakers," according to Bill Kovach and Tom Rosenstiel, authors of *The Elements of Journalism*, for a public that is increasingly bombarded with information.

SCHOLASTIC WATCHDOGS

Student journalists have just as much of an obligation to be sensemakers as do professional journalists. In some ways, student journalists are even more important than their adult counterparts because they have the respect and attention of their peers.

Students might not read a story that is important for teenagers simply because it ran in the local newspaper, they feel disconnected from the publication, or they don't have access to it.

Student media have an important role to play in their schools and communities because young adults are more likely to listen to information coming from their peers.

Student media, on the other hand, commands an audience of peers and allows students to turn to each other for facts and information that are highly relevant to their experiences at school and as young adults.

Because adults are sometimes unaware of the kinds of news topics that matter most to students, scholastic journalists can fill a much-needed gap between the information provided in local newspapers and the information students want and need to know.

Students also have front-row seats to some of the most significant stories in their community. Schools are places in which politics, money, and ideologies often collide. Because many city newspapers are operating with reduced staffs, they may not have enough reporters to consistently cover what happens in each middle or high school.

School board elections, budget cuts, class sizes, grade inflation, and teacher retention are all stories that matter and ones that are likely to go unnoticed by professional media. For example, while local media in Denver, Colorado, covered the 2013 Douglas County School Board election in a rather traditional manner, student journalists at Mountain Vista High School decided to report the story from a unique perspective: teacher satisfaction with the school board. After conducting a teacher survey, both the school news magazine and website printed versions of the survey's results, contextualizing a highly contentious election.

Sometimes, the watchdog approach puts student media on the front lines of national debates. In 2013, leadership at the student newspaper at Neshaminy High School in Pennsylvania made a collective decision to stop using the term "Redskins" in the student newspaper when referring to the school mascot. The *Playwickian* editorial board in October of 2013 argued the term was racist and rooted in emotions of hate, and student editors voted to stop using the word.

Administrators attempted to force the newspaper to reinstate the term, but student editors remained firm, localizing what has become a national debate about rhetoric, racial sensitivity, and the rights and responsibilities of journalists to demonstrate ethical high ground on these kinds of issues.

Why we refuse to publish "The R-Word"

It is one of the most controversial issues in Neshaminy's history. It is a topic that no one wants to discuss, but one that needs to be discussed. It is Neshaminy's nickname, its mascot, its pride. The "Redskin", Neshaminy's long-time moniker, has come under fire from community members for its racist origins and meaning time and time again, all to no avail. Many, if not most, community members and students have shown that they do not wish to have the nickname changed; some don't find it racist (quite the opposite, they think it honors those indigenous to the area), others just want to maintain the tradition. The Playwickian has come to the consensus that the term 'Redskin' is offensive. Whether it's the most basic dictionary definitions , the opinions of many Native Americans, or a more in-depth look at the word's origins, the evidence suggesting that 'Redskin' is a term of honor is severely outweighed by the evidence suggesting that it is a term of hate. It is for these reasons that The Playwickian editorial board has decided it will no longer use the word 'Redskin,' or any derivative such as "'Skins" within its pages in reference to the students or sports teams of Neshaminy High School.

The word 'Redskin' is racist, and very much so. It is not a term of honor, but a term of hate. "Our children look at us when they hear this term with questions on why people would use this hateful word," said Chief Bob Red Hawk, member of the Lenape Nation.

The word itself is ambiguous in its meaning and origin. According to the Oxford English dictionary, it refers to the red face paint used by Native Americans back in the 16th and 17th centuries. Others, like Smithsonian Linguist Ives Goddard, a man now getting press for his research into this issue, believe it a term created by Native Americans to describe themselves as being "red" compared to the "White" Europeans. But in The Washington Post, Goddard himself noted that "you could believe everything in my article" and not agree with using the word. It's also possible that through the process of pejoration, says the Oxford English Dictionary, that the word developed its offensive meaning as time went on. Offended Native Americans commonly cite that the "R-Word" ,as many Natives refer to it, is derived from the time period in which Native Americans were hunted for bounty. In addition to referring to the color of the Natives' skins, 'Redskin' refers to the collecting of their scalped skins during the genocide of the Native peoples. " From the 1600's to the late 1800's cash bounties were posted by both British and U.S. governments for the delivery of "redskins," scalps and body parts," said Clan Mother Ann Dapice, Ph.D, also of the Lenape Nation. While the word started as a term about face-paint, it grew to be much more offensive through pejoration.

Detractors will argue that the word is used with all due respect. But the offensiveness of a word cannot be judged by its intended meaning, but by how it is received.

An Associated Press poll showed that 4/5 of surveyed Native Americans wouldn't change the Washington Redskins mascot, and an Annenberg Public Policy Poll showed 90 percent of the same demographic wouldn't change it.

These numbers may seem low to some, but it must be kept in mind that a sports nickname should not be offending anyone. These numbers could be even higher among local Native Americans, or ones that still celebrate and cherish the Native culture.

Even the most basic dictionary definition of the term describes it as "offensive," "derogatory," or "pejorative." These are also used to describe the "N-word" and other racial slurs. Imagine if Neshaminy had used words of equivalent offensiveness, only for different races. The term 'Negro' is similar to 'Redskin' in its pejorative nature, both started as words without racist charge, but through history, use, and connotation, became words that meant much, much more to the people they describe. It is as unnacceptable to publish the term 'Negro' in casual context as it is 'Redskin'. The 'R-Word' is at least awkward, at most a racist slur. The Playwickian cannot publish it for these reasons. The change is not being encouraged for the sake of political correctness itself, but for the sake of being respectful and fair to an entire race. racist institutions had remained in this areas of society simply because they were time-honored traditions America would be a vastly different place.

Look At It Our Way is the unsigned editorial, which represents the two-thirds view (14 members) of the Editorial Board.

School mascot: point of pride for high school

By Eishna Ranganathan
News Edior

It's a perpetual debate, a national controversy that is tangible at home. The conflict questions the very foundations of Neshaminy pride – the district's mascot, the Redskin. It has been one of the fundamental elements that consistently distinguishes Neshaminy from schools in the vicinity. The term reflects back to the district's heritage; the land on which Native Americans once walked and is depicted as tribute rather than tarnish.

Numerous clubs use the word – yearbook openly displays it, take for example last year's cover. The Playwickian newspaper, one of the most essential aspects of the high school should make it mandatory to properly represent the district via the use of the Redskin. Around Neshaminy, physical education teachers wear sports t-shirts with the Redskins insignia. Simply searching the district website for redskin results in: "Be a Neshaminy Redskin musician, everybody do the redskin rumble, join redskin swimming and diving, redskin marching band." The principal's newsletter is called "Redskin Rumbings." The first image under co-curricular office is "Time will never dim the glory of the Neshaminy Redskins."

A Neshaminy victory is also a Redskin victory. The statement compensates for previous sins to committed upon Indians during America's discovery, employing that there is vast amounts of honor in winning a game being a Redskin. Unlike Wildcats or Tigers, the name had no monotony – it glorifies, not derogates.

Redskin is not racist as it is a representation of the school spirit that Neshaminy represents. At the football games Redskin Nation is not a group of people being racist, they are the students of Neshaminy uniting as one to cheer on the team.

In 2002 Sports Illustrated published a seven-page editorial entitled "The Indian Wars." A poll was conducted amongst Native Americans. In which the following information was gathered:

"Asked if high school and college teams should stop using Indian nicknames, 81 percent of Native American respondents said no. As for pro sports, 83 percent of Native American respondents said teams should not stop using Indian nicknames, mascots, characters and symbols."

Another instance involves a 2004 study; the Annenberg Policy Center at University of Pennsylvania found that when 768 Native Americans were asked "the professional football team in Washington calls itself the Washington Redskins. As a Native American, do you find that name offensive or does it bother you?" Only nine percent declared it "offensive," while one percent had no answer. The other 90 percent said it does not bother them or is insulting in any form.

These statistics make it evident that nationally, when Native American perspectives are accounted for as a whole, the majority finds no slander. A insignificantly-numbered crowd protest and exaggerate the matter.

Ignorance is out of the question; the facts are simple. They are embedded in the achievements of Neshaminy School District and the great strides and progress made carrying the term of redskin. Poquessing, Tawanka and Neshaminy itself are roots of the Native American language leading to the logistic justification of choosing a Redskin mascot.

Neshaminy portrays a 'redskin' in positive light. If the intent is not used in a harmful context, then dispute should not occur. Neshaminy called themselves redskins since the commencement of the school district decades ago. Changing the name would be changing Neshaminy's identity.

It is undeniable that in the past "redskin" has been used in a pejorative sense, but Neshaminy illustrates a genuine example of how, in present day, the attached defamation has disintegrated and is replaced with a high prestige, trumping the past. The shame in changing it exceeds the non-existent shame in keeping it.

Neshaminy creates their own definition of Redskin, apart from the barbaric word that dictionaries classify as. And this is the definition that bestows pride, dignity and accomplishment. The definition that the populace should base their opinions on. The word Neshaminy's context upholds an ageless integrity and a tradition that cannot shatter so easily.

This dissenting point of view represents one-third (7 members) of the Editorial Board.

In 2013, the student newspaper editorial board at Neshaminy High School in Pennsylvania published new policies regarding the paper's use of the term "Redskins."

Their initial editorial explaining their decision is reprinted here, and their arguments strike at the heart of their role as watchdogs:

It is one of the most controversial issues in Neshaminy's history. It is a topic that no one wants to discuss, but one that needs to be discussed. It is Neshaminy's nickname, its mascot, its pride. The

Like professional journalists, scholastic journalists tackle important and even controversial stories. Administrators may sometimes try to censor such stories.

"Redskin," Neshaminy's long-time moniker, has come under fire from community members for its racist origins and meaning time and time again, all to no avail...Even the most basic dictionary definition of the term describes it as "offensive," "derogatory," or "pejorative." These are also used to describe the "N-word" and other racial slurs...The *Playwickian* cannot publish it for these reasons.

The fact that *Playwickian* staffers also published, in full, the minority vote's argument exemplifies responsible, watchdog journalism by presenting a multitude of perspectives on a topic of great public interest. In June 2014, Neshaminy school board officials enacted a new media policy allowing students to remove the term from news articles but not from opinion columns or letters to the editor.

CHAPTER THREE

CENSORSHIP AND SCHOLASTIC PRESS

While scholastic journalism clearly plays an important role in highlighting news and information relevant to students, many scholastic journalists are unable to publish freely. Administrators often misinterpret key legal rulings that allow for censorship in very limited circumstances.

The Student Press Law Center, a nonprofit organization that defends students' First Amendment right to freedom of the press, reports that approximately 2,500 student journalists, teachers, or other people contact it for assistance each year. In many of these cases, a school administrator has prohibited publication of an article, photo, or other media.

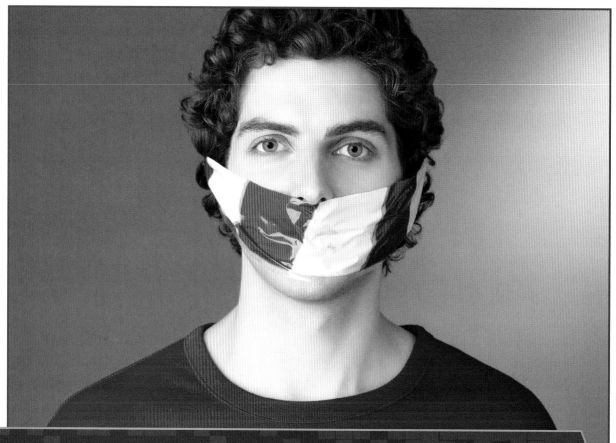

Censorship of student voices goes against the values of democracy and citizenship most schools hope to teach.

Government interference in the right of journalists—whether student or professional—to publish information is rarely constitutional. In the case of student censorship, public school administrators often fear that certain content will cast the school in a negative light or provide fodder for others to criticize the school. This, alone, is not enough reason to legally keep a student from publishing information.

That censorship even occurs (and often) is indication enough that scholastic journalism, and student news, is imperative. Why go to great lengths to censor a publication if it's not important?

CENSORSHIP AND CITIZENSHIP

Censoring student media isn't just bad practice; it's also potentially damaging to young adults' perspectives on citizenship, democracy, diversity of viewpoints, and respect for others. Students who are taught that truthful, accurate information is unacceptable because it might cause offense or discomfort are unlikely to learn respect for differing ideas. What's more, how can we expect students to responsibly participate in a democracy when they are deprived of such a fundamental freedom?

Because all students today are publishers in some way—whether via Facebook, Twitter, blogs, or other media—a thorough understanding of the First Amendment and its role in our democratic society is essential.

Major research by the Knight Foundation in its 2011 *Future of the First Amendment* study shows how perspectives on freedoms of expression, including freedoms of speech and of the press, are changing with the growth of digital media.[6] In their study, they found that students who have had experience in First Amendment instruction are more likely to say newspapers should publish without government interference and that people should be allowed to express unpopular opinions.

A 2013 study by Tufts University also found a link between free expression and civic engagement. To increase voter turnout among young adults, researchers recommended providing students with avenues for participating in civic life. The study makes two recommendations, among others, that relate directly to youth media involvement:

1. "Emphasize youth conducting community research and producing local journalism, with the twin goals of enhancing students' communications skills and making a contribution to the community in light of the severe gap in professional reporting."

2. "Strengthen standards and curricula for digital media literacy and coordinate digital media literacy and civic education."[7]

First Lady Eleanor Roosevelt holds up a copy of the Universal Declaration of Human Rights. The declaration identifies freedom of expression as a central human right.

Arguably, then, students who practice their First Amendment rights to speech, press, religion, petition, or assembly are more likely to value and respect how others exercise those rights. We simply cannot teach what we do not tolerate, so if we wish to teach freedom, democracy, and equality, we must tolerate and even expect that from our students. And in many schools, this begins with the right to publish freely.

A SHORT INTRODUCTION TO MEDIA EFFECTS THEORY

When scholars and researchers talk about "media effects," they are usually referring to the broad impact of mass media consumption in a society. This impact can often be explored by examining changes in religion, politics, culture, and even education. Early media effects studies were based on the notion that media had direct and measurable effects upon those who consumed it.

One of the first researchers to publish about this theory, Walter Lippmann, believed the media could strongly influence public opinion. His 1922 book *Public Opinion* argued that citizens were highly susceptible to propaganda and mass advertisements distributed through the media.

In the late 1940s, researcher Paul Lazarsfeld criticized this belief in direct, transmission-style media effects, finding through a study of voter behavior that the media affected citizens in more limited ways.

Today, thanks to research that began in the late 1960s, many scholars now believe the media has a cumulative effect on consumers. Each person's unique situation, family, upbringing, education, socioeconomic status, and even geographic location will help determine whether the media has powerful and significant effects or minimal and limited effects on their beliefs and perceptions.

The importance of free expression for all humans, and not just adults in a democracy, is a global cause. The United Nations' Universal Declaration of Human Rights explicitly advocates for freedom of expression across race, culture, politics, and country: "Everyone has the right to freedom of opinion and expression; this right includes freedom to hold opinions without interference and to seek, receive and impart information and ideas through any media and regardless of frontiers."

CHAPTER

CHALLENGES TO TRADITIONAL JOURNALISM

One of the greatest challenges facing traditional journalism, and one that threatens to undermine a profession embedded in the very fabric of our country, is the rise of self-publishing. Blogging platforms, social media accounts, and the ease of website creation have turned millions of citizens into citizen journalists—self-proclaimed publishers of opinion, information, truth, and spin.

As technology has made it easier, faster, and cheaper to publish words, images, and graphics, the news industry has turned to citizen journalists to supplement or even replace the work of professional journalists. Major publications are laying off reporters and photographers, arguing they can do more with less because citizens and social media will fill in the gap.

WHO IS A PROFESSIONAL JOURNALIST?

Defining who, exactly, is a professional journalist has major implications. For example, journalists are typically protected by law against retribution for certain types of content. Private citizens who publish that same content may not receive the same protection.

In 2011, for example, a blogger in Montana lost a multimillion-dollar lawsuit for calling an Oregon lawyer corrupt on her website. The federal judge ruled that Crystal Cox was not a journalist, and therefore, laws meant to protect journalists from having to reveal sources in defamation cases did not apply to her or her case.[8] Student journalists who use anonymous sources might face similar challenges to disclose sources or provide confidential information.

In 2013, the Senate Judiciary Committee passed a federal shield law, the Free Flow of Information Act. Though still pending in Congress at the time of this writing, the law, if passed, would protect even college journalists and bloggers from being forced to reveal anonymous sources.

This trend, though alarming in many ways, is not entirely a death knell for journalism. Those in the news industry have been forced to rethink their business approach, the quality of their product, and how they interact with the public. In some instances, the result is a better, more targeted news product. For other publications, the pendulum swings in the opposite direction—toward entertainment, hype, and other quick-selling, high-profit topics.

PROTECTING THOSE WHO RELEASE INFORMATION

The question of who should be protected for revealing important information is made even more complicated when the information disclosed has grave political and national security implications. In the history of the United States, mainstream media has generally published news of any political leaks or missteps. The *New York Times*, for example, first published the Pentagon Papers in 1971. The papers detailed the United States' controversial involvement in the Vietnam War. The next year, the

In addition to traditional newspapers, Edward Snowden turned to the website WikiLeaks to publish classified government documents he obtained while working as a contractor for the National Security Agency.

Washington Post first published accounts of the Watergate scandal, an ongoing coverup of President Richard Nixon and his administration's involvement in illegal wiretapping, burglary, and money transfers.

In both cases, the whistleblowers, or people who expose misconduct or illegal activity in an organization, brought their information to the mainstream press. Today, whistleblowers are turning to alternative and online media to release information.

WikiLeaks, a website that publishes leaks and classified information, is one example of how technology has changed the way sensitive information is shared with the public. Media organizations and governments have argued for years whether founder Julian Assange qualifies as a journalist, with some going so far as to say he is a terrorist deserving of criminal prosecution.[9]

Similarly, former National Security Agency employee Edward Snowden in 2013 leaked documents about a secret global surveillance program to British and United States newspapers. Called both a whistleblower and a traitor, Snowden has repeatedly said his only goal was to inform the public about suspect government actions.[10]

Is anyone with information a journalist? Is any platform that provides such information considered news? These are the pressing questions of our time, and they cannot easily be answered. As technology complicates our perspectives on who is a journalist and what is news, journalism education provides a much-needed starting point for all students.

CHAPTER FIVE

WHY JOURNALISM EDUCATION MATTERS

Today, public education is a moving target. Changing federal policies, budget limitations, and new standards initiatives have left scholastic journalism in flux. Many schools are cutting student media because they are uncertain of how scholastic journalism curriculum fits into a larger framework of testable, standardized skill sets. To be clear, journalism education epitomizes the skills administrators and policymakers hope students will develop before entering college or the professional world.

According to the Partnership for 21st Century Skills, today's educational system approach should accomplish three goals:[11]

1. "Prepare all students to participate effectively as citizens." As discussed earlier, students who participate in journalism often develop a greater appreciation for what it means to be an active citizen. One cannot be a great reporter or watchdog without understanding how government works, and journalists tend to demonstrate a curiosity for current events and political issues. What's more, journalism offers a platform for the public and professionals to discuss the most important events and ideas of the day.

2. "Reimagine citizenship from a global perspective." Students who are engaged in their community and who participate in civic life through journalism are likely to be more aware of the larger civic and social forces at work in the world. Context is essential for any fact-finding mission, and student journalists learn to understand the world as they seek out the best, most accurate information available.

3. "Focus on digital citizenship." Student journalists understand the benefits and limitations of a digital world. They know just how powerful online technology can be because they harness it on a regular basis to disseminate accurate, thorough information. As part of the learning curve inherent in journalism, students are also likely to develop a keen awareness of the potential pitfalls of digital communication. This, in turn, creates savvier, more literate media consumers and producers.

Most importantly, scholastic journalism provides a rich, laboratory-style setting in which to accomplish these goals and more. Under the guidance of trained and experienced faculty advisers, students can learn to be responsible participants and contributors in a digital age.

Scholastic journalism also stands up to other contemporary standards initiatives. The Common Core State Standards initiative, for example, recognizes the need for students to read, process, and create informational texts. In fact, outcomes of the Common Core initiative directly relate to students' abilities to process information—a key outcome of scholastic journalism programs. The standards describe the habits of college- and career-ready students and embody the skills scholastic journalists practice on a daily basis:

> They habitually perform the critical reading necessary to pick carefully through the staggering amount of information available today in print and digitally. They actively seek the wide, deep, and thoughtful engagement with high-quality literary and informational texts that builds knowledge, enlarges experience, and broadens worldviews. They reflexively demonstrate the cogent reasoning and use of evidence that is essential to both private deliberation and responsible citizenship in a democratic republic.[12]

Schools with career and technical education programs find that student media, especially broadcast programs, exemplify requirements under the arts, audio/visual technology, and communications cluster. In short, the argument that journalism education is not standards-based is clearly misinformed.

While it is easy to see how journalism education satisfies national standards, there is an even more pressing reason why journalism education is a vital part of a well-rounded scholastic experience: our students will never live in a world without media.

Media and technology will dictate the most significant cultural, social, and political decisions of our time. Access to information, how that information is conveyed and its truth value, and whether anyone bothers to connect the dots between the multitude of stories told across all media, will forever shape our reality. As Student Press Law Center executive director Frank LoMonte wrote:

"The right of students to express themselves in the student media without fear and intimidation has been the concern of civil-liberties advocates and journalism educators, but those communities cannot change the authoritarian mindset of schools by themselves. Progress will come—and it *will* come—with the recognition that valuing student voices is an education reform without which other reforms are incomplete."[13]

Providing students with the tools to sift fact from fiction, to use media to empower themselves and others, and to demand factual, relevant

Today's students will never live in a world without media. Scholastic journalism allows students to create a variety of media and to experience how the production and dissemination of news impacts society.

information is the most critical role schools can play in our highly connected world. To do anything less is a disservice to students and to their future.

To put it simply, journalism and media education must no longer be an elective, extracurricular endeavor. It must be the platform from which we empower our students to engage in the world in the most constructive, enlightened, civically aware ways possible.

A MEDIA LITERATE APPROACH

It's clear now that the skills required to be a journalist are starting to greatly overlap the skills necessary to be a responsible, informed citizen. News producers and news consumers are no longer separate, mutually exclusive entities that interact in only a linear fashion.

Instead, the flow of production and consumption is much more circular. Many citizens produce media, and all citizens consume it. Sometimes, in response to the media they consume, citizens become producers by responding via whatever media is available to them: website comments, YouTube videos, or social media posts.

Understanding this dynamic and the unique steps consumers can take to empower themselves in a digital media world is a necessary part of a well-rounded secondary education. To accomplish these tasks, many schools are now teaching media literacy.

Defined simply, media literacy is a set of skills—or competencies—that allows consumers and producers of media to analyze the information given, evaluate how accurate it is, and respond in responsible ways that further dialogue, promote truth, and hold citizens responsible.

EXPLORING MEDIA LITERACY

As a class, in teams, or individually, complete the following exercises to learn more about the basics of media literacy and your own consumption habits. Because media literacy is a process, you're likely to find many different types of articles that approach this concept in myriad ways. After tracking your own media consumption habits, you'll be able to identify with what kind of media you spend most of your time. Then, consider how you might broaden your media habits by experiencing different kinds of media.

1. Use an Internet search engine, such as Google, to find an article that discusses media literacy. Read and summarize the main points of the article.

2. Track what kind of media you use in a twenty-four-hour period to find out what your media habits look like.

3. Pick one of the vocabulary words from the glossary and search for news articles or educational readings about the concept. Find and share a real-life example of the concept with your classmates.

Media literacy is not a theory—it is an ongoing process that helps citizens understand how mass media systems work even as they change over time. These systems include news, entertainment, and advertising media. The National Association for Media Literacy Education explains media literacy in the following way: "Media literacy empowers people to be both critical thinkers and creative producers of an increasingly wide range of messages using image, language, and sound. It is the skillful application of literacy skills to media and technology messages."[14]

To be media literate requires students to process any kind of media by first accepting a few realities:

1. Media messages affect our perspectives on all things (society, culture, religion, politics, education, morals, etc.).
2. Media messages are often reflections of the media systems in which they were created.
3. Media messages reflect versions of reality and fantasy.
4. Media messages often convey values and ideologies.

Walter Lippmann, one of the great American journalists of the early 1900s, believed that distorted or inaccurate news was a central problem in a democracy.

5. How we interpret messages depends on a variety of personal, social, economic, and cultural factors.

6. Media messages and systems often reflect and perpetuate the power dimensions of our society.

7. Media messages often conflate truth and fact.

These are just a few of the main concepts of media literacy, but they represent the heart of what it means to be an informed, active, empowered media consumer. It's important, however, to recognize that these realities do not automatically assume all media are bad or that all media influences are negative. To imagine that all media producers intend to manipulate or spin information is much too simplistic and is likely to result in news consumers becoming cynical instead of critical about the information they seek.

Researchers used to think that the effects of media consumption were strong and direct. This "hypodermic needle" approach assumed that citizens read, watched, or listened to media and immediately internalized the effects of whatever content they consumed. Now we know that this theory is inaccurate. How media content and consumption change the ways we think and behave is much more subtle. In fact, without a concerted effort to understand how media affects our lives, we may not even recognize how it's changing us until it's too late.

Media literacy is a natural companion to journalism education because of the expectation that responsible media consumers no doubt contribute and produce their own media on occasion. Remember, even the social media posts, blogs, photos, or links students publish every day while interacting with friends online are a type of media.

Of course, every student can benefit from becoming media literate because so much of the way we communicate today is facilitated through media. But scholastic journalists can also benefit from media literacy education. The more student journalists know about how media systems work, their history, effects, benefits, and limitations, the more proficient communicators they will become. Journalism is, after all, storytelling. And to tell a compelling, contextual, accurate story requires a deep understanding of media systems.

GLOSSARY

censorship The suppression of ideas and information, generally by state or government officials or other authority figures.

Common Core State Standards A set of K–12 education standards designed to standardize state education standards through voluntary adoption.

digital immigrant A person who is relatively new to the digital world and is building competency in digital skills such as using the Internet.

digital native A person who was born into the age of the Internet and has used digital skills from a young age.

First Amendment The first section of the Bill of Rights and first amendment to the U.S. Constitution, which guarantees the freedoms of speech, press, religion, petition, and assembly.

gatekeepers A term used to refer to those in the media business who decide what information is published.

hypodermic needle theory A media effects theory that suggests the media affects users in immediate, powerful, noticeable ways. This theory is outdated and is less accurate than other theories that posit media's effects are more subtle and nuanced.

information overload Used to describe the overwhelming influx of information available in the digital age, largely as a result of self-publishing and search engines.

media literacy The process by which media consumers learn to critically examine, analyze and respond to mass media.

netizen A citizen who uses the Internet for mostly civic purposes.

sensemakers A description used to refer to journalists because of their responsibility to filter immense amounts of information into a readable (or viewable) story for consumers.

watchdog A descriptor for journalists who uphold their responsibility to scrutinize government activity, present minority opinions, and provide a voice to those generally underrepresented in mass media.

whistleblower A person who alerts authorities to government or corporate wrong-doing.

Center for Media Literacy
22837 Pacific Coast Highway, #472
Malibu, CA 90265
(310) 804-3985
Website: http://www.medialit.org
The Center for Media Literacy provides many educational resources and
    updated research on media literacy education.

The Center for News Literacy
N4029 Melville Library
Stony Brook University
Stony Brook, NY 11794-3384
(631) 632-7637
Website: http://www.centerfornewsliteracy.org
The Center for News Literacy provides lessons and other curricular material
    related to news literacy.

Journalism Education Association
Kansas State University
103 Kedzie Hall
Manhattan, KS 66506-1505
(866) 532-5532
Website: http://www.jea.org
The Journalism Education Association is the largest professional association
    for secondary journalism teachers and scholastic media advisers.

Media Education Lab
Harrington School of Communication and Media
University of Rhode Island
Davis Hall
Kingston, RI 02881
Website: http://www.mediaeducationlab.com

Media Education Lab provides scholarship and community service aimed at educating students about digital literacy.

National Association for Media Literacy Education (NAMLE)
10 Laurel Hill Drive
Cherry Hill, NJ 08003
(888) 775-2652
Website: http://www.namle.net
NAMLE is a national membership organization dedicated to helping citizens of all ages learn media literacy skills.

WEBSITES

Because of the changing nature of Internet links, Rosen Publishing has developed an online list of websites related to the subject of this book. This site is updated regularly. Please use this link to access the list:

http://www.rosenlinks.com/MEDL/Ethic

Bauerlein, Mark. *The Digital Divide: Arguments for and Against Facebook, Google, Texting, and the Age of Social Networking*. London, England: Penguin Books, 2011.

Brock, George. *Out of Print: Newspapers, Journalism, and the Business of News in the Digital Age*. London, England: Kogan Page Limited, 2013.

Folkenflik, David. *Page One: Inside the New York Times and the Future of Journalism*. Digital edition. PublicAffairs, 2011.

Hobbs, Renee. *Digital and Media Literacy: Connecting Culture and Classroom*. Thousand Oaks, CA: Corwin, 2011.

Jenkins, Henry. *Convergence Culture: Where Old & New Media Collide*. New York, NY: New York University, 2006.

Kovach, Bill, and Tom Rosenstiel. *Blur: How to Know What's True in the Age of Information Overload*. New York, NY: Bloomsbury, 2010.

Kovach, Bill, and Tom Rosenstiel. *The Elements of Journalism*. New York, NY: Three Rivers, 2007.

Mihailidis, Paul. *News Literacy: Global Perspectives for the Newsroom and the Classroom*. New York, NY: Peter Lang, 2011.

Shirky, Clay. *The Power of Organizing Without Organizations*. New York, NY: Penguin Books, 2008.

Standage, Tom. *Writing on the Wall: Social Media–the First 2,000 Years*. New York, NY: Bloomsbury, 2013.

Thompson, Clive. *Smarter Than You Think: How Technology Is Changing Our Minds for the Better*. New York, NY: Penguin, 2013.

END NOTES

1. The American Presidency Project. "Remarks on the 20th Anniversary of the Voice of America." Retrieved May 18, 2014 (http://www.presidency.ucsb.edu/ws/?pid=9075).

2. Pew Research Internet Project. "Teens Fact Sheet." Retrieved February 19, 2014 (http://www.pewinternet.org/Commentary/2012/April/Pew-Internet-Teens.aspx).

3. Kaiser Family Foundation. "Generation M2: Media in the Lives of 8- to 18-Year-Olds." Retrieved February 19, 2014 (http://kff.org/other/event/generation-m2-media-in-the-lives-of).

4. Mihailidis, Paul, Eivind Michaelsen, and Kristin Berg. "Exploring Mobile Information Habits of University Students Around the World." *A Tethered World*, October 2, 2012. Retrieved February 19, 2014 (http://tetheredworld.wordpress.com).

5. Kamiya, Gary. "Iraq: Why the Media Failed." Salon.com, April 10, 2007. Retrieved February 19, 2014 (http://www.salon.com/2007/04/10/media_failure).

6. Dautrich, Kenneth. *Future of the First Amendment*. Knightfoundation.org. Retrieved February 19, 2014 (http://www.knightfoundation.org/media/uploads/publication_pdfs/Future-of-the-First-Amendment-full-cx2.pdf).

7. Commission on Youth Voting and Civic Knowledge. *All Together Now: Collaboration and Innovation for Youth Engagement*. Civicyouth.org, 2013. Retrieved February 19, 2014 (http://www.civicyouth.org/wp-content/uploads/2013/09/CIRCLE-youthvoting-individualPages.pdf).

8. Harlow, Summer. "U.S. Court Rules Oregon Blogger Not a Journalist." *Journalism in the Americas* blog, December 7, 2011. Knight Center for Journalism in the Americas. Retrieved February 19, 2014 (https://knightcenter.utexas.edu/blog/us-court-rules-oregon-blogger-not-journalist).

9. Gant, Scott. "Why Julian Assange Is a Journalist." Salon.com, December 20, 2010. Retrieved February 19, 2014 (http://www.salon.com/2010/12/20/wikileaks_gant_journalism).

[10] Greenwald, Glenn, Ewen MacAskill, and Laura Poitras. "Ed Snowden: The Whistleblower Behind the NSA Surveillance Revelations." Guardian.com, June 9, 2013. Retrieved February 19, 2014 (http://www.theguardian.com/world/2013/jun/09/edward-snowden-nsa-whistleblower-surveillance).

[11] Partnership for 21st Century Skills. *Reimagining Citizenship for the 21st Century.* Retrieved February 19, 2014 (http://www.p21.org/storage/documents/Reimagining_Citizenship_for_21st_Century_webversion.pdf).

[12] Common Core State Standards Initiative. "English Language Arts Standards." Retrieved February 19, 2014 (http://www.corestandards.org/ELA-Literacy).

[13] LoMonte, Frank. "Two New Reports on Civic Engagement in Schools Identify a Central Role for Scholastic Journalism Skills." Student Press Law Center, October 13, 2013. Retrieved February 19, 2014 (http://www.splc.org/wordpress/?p=5838).

[14] National Association for Media Literacy Education. "Media Literacy Defined." Retrieved February 19, 2014 (http://namle.net/publications/media-literacy-definitions).

INDEX

ABOUT THE AUTHOR

Megan Fromm is an assistant professor at Boise State University and faculty for the Salzburg Academy on Media & Global Change, a summer media literacy study-abroad program. She is also the professional support director for the Journalism Education Association.

Fromm received her Ph.D. in 2010 from the Philip Merrill College of Journalism at the University of Maryland. Her dissertation analyzed how news media frame student First Amendment court cases, particularly those involving freedom of speech and press. Her work and teaching centers on media law, scholastic journalism, media literacy, and media and democracy. She has also worked as a journalist and high school journalism teacher. Fromm has taught at Johns Hopkins University, Towson University, the University of Maryland, and the Newseum.

As a working journalist, Fromm won numerous awards, including the Society of Professional Journalists Sunshine Award and the Colorado Friend of the First Amendment Award. Fromm worked in student media through high school and college and interned at the Student Press Law Center in 2004. Her career in journalism began at Grand Junction High School (Grand Junction, Colorado), where she was a reporter and news editor for the award-winning student newspaper, the *Orange & Black*.

PHOTO CREDITS

Cover (people at table) © iStockphoto.com/skynesher; cover (apps icons) © iStockphoto.com/scanrail; cover background (receding screens) © iStockphoto.com/Danil Melek; cover and interior pages (pixel pattern) © iStockphoto.com/hellena13; p. 4-5 Oleg Golovnev/Shutterstock.com; p. 9 Jetta Productions/Photodisc/Thinkstock; p. 11 JuliusKielaitis/Shutterstock.com; p. 14 De Agostini/Getty Images; p. 16 Illustration by Ari Charnoff, Dore Feith, Stuart Krantz, and Jonathan Reem, The Lion's Tale, Charles E. Smith Jewish Day School, MD; p. 18 Purestock/Getty Images; p. 20: Staff, The Playwickian, Neshaminy High School, PA; p. 21: Nivedha Meyyappan, HiLite, Carmel High School, IN; p. 24 Image Source/Digital Vision/Getty Images; p. 26 Fotosearch/Archive Photos/Getty Images; p. 29 Walter Bennett/Time & Life Pictures/Getty Images; p. 31 Gary Miller/FilmMagic/Getty Images; p. 35 omgimages/iStock/Thinkstock; p. 38 Keystone/Hulton Archive/Getty Images.

Designer: Nicole Russo; Editor: Nicholas Croce